Puffers
Guthrie Hutton

The Hillhead Basin, Kirkintilloch, was often crowded with boats because many puffermen lived in the area. This picture, showing two puffers and two scows (the unpowered barge from which puffers evolved) was taken from the canal steamer *Gipsy Queen* in July 1936, two years before the wooden bridge in the foreground was replaced by a steel swing bridge.

1

Ross & Marshall's *Sealight*, was a 154 ton, steel-hulled vessel built at Greenock in 1930 by George Brown & Co. Her dimensions - 85 feet long, 19 feet 6 inches beam and drawing just over 9 feet - allowed her to use the Crinan Canal, but not the Forth & Clyde Canal with its smaller locks and slightly shallower water. She was broken up at Troon in 1963.

ACKNOWLEDGEMENTS

The pictures in this book are from a private collection and many of these were photographed by the late Dan McDonald, a great enthusiast who wrote what is arguably the definitive book on puffers in 1976. His work to research and record ships' details has enriched the Clyde's heritage. Despite our best efforts we could not find any family member from whom to obtain permission to use Dan's images and hope no offence is caused by presenting them in this way. A large archive of his pictures is held by the Ballast Trust whose co-operation is appreciated.

I must thank library staffs in Glasgow, Greenock, Kirkintilloch and Dundee for their help. Craig Osborne supplied some invaluable material as did William B. Black who let me quote statistics from his excellent research paper *The Glasgow Canal Shipbuilders*. I should also pay tribute to my late friend Ian Bowman who wrote a splendid and detailed account of the Kirkintilloch puffers. My thanks also go to Tommy Lawton for the picture on the left of page 48 and to Peter Baillie for sharing his memories of working on puffers as a young man.

I am grateful too to the puffermen who I met in my younger days, especially Walter Kerr of the *Saxon*, and Davie Craig and Charlie Cornish of the *Starlight*, all of whom made a big impact and stirred my enthusiasm. Davie's lesson in rope throwing, imparted one Saturday at the Queen's Dock in Glasgow, has stuck with me to this day.

INTRODUCTION

The first practical application of steam power to marine propulsion was on a tug named *Charlotte Dundas*. Developed by engineer William Symington, she towed two other boats along the Forth & Clyde Canal on a day in March 1803 when the headwind was so strong it prevented any horse-drawn traffic from going west. It was a triumph, but fears that the large stern–mounted paddle wheel would damage the canal put a stop to further trials. With development of his invention sidelined, Symington's fortunes slumped. He even had to contend with an American rival, Robert Fulton, who claimed a world first when he sailed his *Clermont* on the Hudson River in 1807.

The publicity Fulton generated also ignored the contribution of another Scottish pioneer, Henry Bell, who began a service on the Clyde in 1812 with his new steam boat, *Comet*. She had side–mounted paddle wheels, a design that was quickly adopted by other shipbuilders on the Clyde and elsewhere. Some paddlers were eventually permitted on the canal but they were never popular, mainly because locks had to be filled and emptied twice to pass both the tug and its barge. Development stagnated for many years, but as competition from the railways grew canal users had to find a way of competing.

Built at Port Glasgow in 1866 *Elizabeth* was, for a time, owned by Rothesay timber merchant George Halliday. She is seen here at the coal pier at Brodick, which puffers used because it was cheaper than·the main pier.

The solution came in 1856 when screw propulsion was fitted to an existing canal lighter, the *Thomas*, at the canal company's Hamilton Hill boatyard. This was an immediate success and other owners quickly adapted their craft. The following year a brand new propeller-driven, steam-powered, iron-hulled lighter was launched at Kelvin Dock, Maryhill. Named *Glasgow* she is regarded as the first puffer.

The puffers' origins as barges made them an ideal shape for carrying bulk cargo in confined waters, and small canal-side boatyards continued the process of refining and perfecting the design well into the twentieth century. From the earliest days puffers also ventured out of the canal and different specifications evolved to deal with the demands of deep sea, estuarial or canal work. So well suited were they to the tight little harbours of the Clyde and the West Coast that they replaced the sailing vessels - sloops (sometimes known as gabbarts), smacks and schooners that had hitherto been the principal coastal trading craft.

As the early canal influence diminished the boats became known as 'Clyde Puffers'. A large number were built at riverside yards and some of these were made to suit the larger dimensions of the Crinan Canal. Some boats formed part of small company fleets, others were owner operated and a number worked out of east coast ports. After the Second World War, steam prevailed for a while but in the 1950s and 60s the classic puffer shape began to give way to diesel coasters which, although they retained some puffer features, were too large for either canal. With such vessels, coastal shipping could (and perhaps should) have continued to play an important role in the transport of freight around Scotland, but competition from roads and ferries, built and supported by public funds, brought about their demise in the 1990s.

Nelson was one of many puffers which were introduced to the world with a side-on launch into the Forth & Clyde Canal. She was a classic canal-built puffer; 81 tons, 66 feet long, 18 feet in the beam and drawing 6 foot 3 inches of water, dimensions tailored to the size of the canal locks. She was launched from J. & J. Hay's yard at Kirkintilloch on a May evening in 1893 - Hay's launched more such boats than any other canalside yard. It was, as the picture shows, very wet but a large crowd watched as the iron–hulled vessel slid into the canal sending a wave of water onto the towpath to drench anyone standing too close. Intended for Hay's North of Ireland coasting trade, her strong construction served her well five years later when she went aground in Belfast Lough. Despite fears that she would be a total loss, she was salvaged and remained in Hay's fleet until being sold in 1924.

The three boats lined up in this picture of Bowling Basin are thought to be, from the left, *Hannibal*, *Hero* and *Caesar*. They belonged to J. & J. Hay and were all involved in accidents on the canal. *Hannibal* sank to the west of Kirkintilloch in 1893, *Caesar* went down near Maryhill in 1897 and in the same year *Hero* sank in Lock 4 between Falkirk and Grangemouth when her boiler blew up, killing the skipper and mate, and badly injuring the lock keeper. Incidents like these, which all happened in the confined waters of the canal, highlight the dangers faced by puffermen. They regarded their vessels as good sea boats, able to take rough water like a bobbing cork, but despite this the attrition rate among these small vessels was very high.

Victor was the third boat - after *Norman* and *Hero* - to be built at J. & J. Hay's Kirkintilloch Townhead yard in 1896. She was launched in November of that year and was the yard's last iron-hulled boat. At 44 tons, she was intended for work in confined waters, but in response to Admiralty requirements was converted for coastal work during the First World War. She is seen here at Temple on the Forth & Clyde Canal in 1932. Behind her is the brand new steel bascule bridge built by Sir William Arrol & Co. to replace the earlier wooden bridge which spanned Lock 27 (behind the camera). The realignment of Bearsden Road cut Robinson Dunn's timber yard in two and separated the little wharf where *Victor* is tied up from the main part of the yard. *Victor* was eventually scrapped at Kirkintilloch in 1944.

Early boats were called steam lighters, a term which originated before the advent of steam power when horse–drawn canal barges were known as either scows or lighters. Later horse–drawn craft were commonly described as scows while the steam vessels were called lighters. They also became popularly known as puffers because they had non-condensing steam engines which expelled exhaust fumes out of the funnel with a puffing sound. The term stuck long after such engines were superseded and the funnels stopped puffing.

The first *Druid*, was a 92 ton steel-hulled vessel built at Kirkintilloch in 1899 but lost only a few years later. She was replaced in 1905 with another *Druid*, which seemed to have inherited her predecessor's luck when she went ashore at Fair Head near Ballycastle in 1912. Hay's, however, sent out a rescue squad who made her seaworthy again. During the First World War she worked at Scapa Flow for the Admiralty and in 1919 she returned to the coastal trade. She is seen here in Queen's Dock, Glasgow, in 1949, six years before being sold. A third *Druid*, a 197 ton motor vessel, was launched or, more exactly, hoisted into the water by crane at Papendracht, Holland, in 1959. Three years later she capsized in bad weather off Preston Bar in the Ribble estuary and was lost along with three of her five-man crew.

The closure of the upper Forth ports, including Grangemouth, during the First World War brought most canal trade to a halt and so J. & J. Hay converted some boats to coastal work. One of these, the *Dane*, which was launched in 1903, was also renamed *Saxon*, the third of their fleet to bear the name. She survived the war, but sank on a December night in 1925 after being hit by the Belfast collier *Melissa* off Princes Pier, Greenock. The crew of three was saved, but skipper Allan McLean died later in hospital. *Saxon* was bought where she lay by Finlay and Walter Kerr of Millport who raised her and operated her between the Isle of Cumbrae and the mainland, principally to bring coal to the island from Troon. She was used as the *Vital Spark* in 1965 for the BBC Scotland series in which Roddy MacMillan first played Para Handy. The role was originally performed on television in 1959/60 by Duncan MacRae.

Saxon is seen here as the *Vital Spark* on the beach at Lochranza, Arran. The broad, if not exactly flat, bottoms of puffers enabled them to be beached on soft shores although crews did not relish doing this at unfamiliar places where a stray rock could damage the hull. Adverse tides could also leave a boat stranded for days. A trick puffermen used to re-float a beached vessel was to lower the anchor on to their small boat, row out and drop it in deeper water. They could then pull themselves off the beach with the winch when the puffer started to gain buoyancy. In the other picture *Saxon*, as *Vital Spark*, is at Inveraray pier with a mock fund-raising mine - used as a television prop - in the foreground. After her starring role, *Saxon* was put up for sale, but no-one bought her and she was scrapped in 1967.

The first time a puffer appeared on screen was in the 1954 Ealing comedy film, *The Maggie*. Based on the Para Handy stories, the film told of a roguish skipper and his crew obtaining a cargo by deception. They then head out from the Glasgow docks, through the Crinan Canal and on to the Western Isles, where the boat ends up on the rocks and they have to jettison the cargo to save her. This was all familiar puffer territory with the activities of the crew and fate of their vessel almost documentary-like in their accuracy. One of the most memorable moments came when the boat stuck on the tunnel carrying the Glasgow Subway under the Clyde. For this scene, a full scale mock-up was built on a barge and floated into position. It is seen here ready for filming in September 1953.

Two of Hay's 72 ton coasting vessels, *Boer* and *Inca*, were used as *The Maggie*. *Inca* was built at the Townhead yard at Kirkintilloch in 1938 and *Boer* followed in 1941. Despite the three year gap the two were identical in every respect. *Boer* is seen here, in an undated picture, beside Hay's repair slip at Southbank Road, Kirkintilloch. The slipway remained in use for sixteen years after building work ceased at Townhead, but the canal's closure in 1963 forced the company to abandon their Kirkintilloch base. *Inca* and *Boer* were broken up two years later.

The *Na Kiel* began life as *Cretan*, a 92 ton coasting vessel, built at Kirkintilloch in 1910 by J. & J. Hay. She spent the First World War on charter to the Admiralty at Cromarty before returning to the west coast. She sank in Loch na Keal, off the west coast of Mull, in January 1939 and was written off as a constructive wreck. Sold where she lay, she was refloated by her new owners and renamed *Na Kiel*, presumably to reflect the loch's name, but with a different spelling. She is seen here in 1950, the year before she was broken up, with a canvas dodger to protect the helmsman from the elements; puffermen were only provided with the luxury of a wheel house comparatively late in the story of these vessels.

After losing their first *Cretan* the Hays lost little time in replacing her with another boat of the same name, launched at Kirkintilloch in early December 1939. Being war time, there was no ceremony, but a large crowd still gathered and the yard foreman had to ask them to be quiet so that the men whose job it was to sever the ropes holding the boat could hear his instructions. On the count of three they swung their axes and *Cretan* (2) entered the water. In an echo of what happened to the first *Cretan*, she sank in a storm in late November 1954 off Bogany Point at the entrance to Rothesay Bay. Part of her cargo of coal was taken off before she could be raised and put back into service. She is seen here at Brodick in 1957.

Soon after her launch in 1901, the first *Moor* was made available, along with four scows, to take 1,000 people on an outing from Kirkintilloch to Cadder. With some 300 people on deck, the unballasted boat rolled alarmingly on leaving the jetty and passengers jumped for their lives as she slewed across the canal and crashed into a scow loaded with picnickers from Glasgow. It was an inauspicious start and she met an untimely end, while on contract to the Admiralty. Two days before Christmas 1915 she was overwhelmed by high seas while crossing the bar at the mouth of the Tay. Neither the trawler, whose crew saw the puffer hit by a giant wave, nor the Broughty Ferry lifeboat found any survivors. The second *Moor* was launched in 1925 and was the largest boat built up to that time at Hay's Kirkintilloch yard. Seen here at Glasgow's Princes Dock, she had a less eventful life than her predecessor and ended life as a hulk after being de-engined in 1956.

The second *Turk* was a 70 ton vessel launched at Kirkintilloch on Christmas Day, 1929. Six months later, on the evening of 17 June, she arrived from Ardentinny at Princes Dock, Glasgow, with timber - often an unstable cargo. While unloading the following morning, the vessel heeled over, without warning, against the quay wall and sank. Acting with speed and skill the dockside crane man managed to lift off the three man crew before the boat went under. She was refloated two weeks later and went back into service. She is seen here in 1958 across the river in Queen's Dock with her near sister, *Slav*, which was launched in 1932. Both boats have just been loaded with coal, hence the uniform angle of their derricks which have been parked out of the way of the dockside hoist. *Slav* was the last puffer to be repaired at Hay's Kirkintilloch slip in November 1961, just over a year before the canal's closure and a couple of years before both she and *Turk* were scrapped.

J. & J. Hay and J. Hay & Sons (as the company was known between 1921 and 1956) typically named their boats after tribes or warrior peoples. The only one to be named *Texan* was launched at Kirkintilloch in 1937. Coincidentally that was the same year that *The Texas Rangers* starring Fred MacMurray and Jack Oakie appeared at the town's Black Bull cinema - could that have inspired the name? Within a couple of years of her launch the Second World War broke out and she was based at Crombie on the Forth, working for the Admiralty as a fleet tender. She is seen here on more peaceable pursuits at Rothesay in 1960, four years before she was broken up.

A launch at the Hay's Kirkintilloch yard was a great occasion for the town, attracting big crowds. The yard was adjacent to the Townhead Bridge which provided a splendid vantage point, but as the *Kirkintilloch Herald* pointed out in November 1934, the old wooden bridge, which had been replaced in 1933 by a steel swing bridge, would have been unable to bear the weight of the throng that turned up to watch the launch of the 93 ton *Tuscan*. Converted to burning oil fuel in 1948, she is seen here at Queen's Dock the following year. In June 1955 she tried for two days to land a cargo of coal at Arran but was thwarted by bad weather. When the skipper tried again he was caught by a freak storm off Dhunan Point in Brodick Bay and *Tuscan* was swamped by the heavy seas. The crew took to their dinghy, but when it capsized, they had to be rescued by the steamer *Kildonan* which had been tied up at Brodick Pier.

Although J. Hay & Sons had a long working relationship with Scott & Company at Bowling, they surprised the puffer world when they decided to have two boats designed and built by them. Launched in 1939 the *Anzac* and *Lascar*, were at 99 tons, larger than anything previously built at Kirkintilloch, although still of dimensions to suit the canal. Both were converted to diesel in 1959: *Anzac* is seen here in her original steam mode and the diesel driven *Lascar* is seen leaving Queen's Dock. Not only did these boats create a stir because of where they were built, but their design was adopted by the Admiralty during the Second World War for a number of fleet tenders known as Victualling Inshore Craft, or VIC's for short. Most of these were built at small English yards and some found their way to Scotland after the war.

Two wartime VIC craft were built at Kirkintilloch for the Admiralty. One of these, VIC 18, was launched in 1942 and after her war service joined Hay's fleet as *Spartan*, the third of the company's boats to bear the name. She is seen here in her original steam-driven shape at Cairnbaan on the Crinan Canal and passing Yoker Power Station after she had been converted to diesel in 1961. The space saved by replacing steam machinery with diesel was used to provide better crew accommodation, evident from the four portholes at the after end. *Spartan* continued to work until 1980 before being laid up at Bowling. In 1982 she was sold for £1 by her then owners, Glenlight Shipping, to a group calling itself the West of Scotland Boat Museum Association. They formed a partnership the following year with the Irvine Development Corporation to establish the Scottish Maritime Museum, with *Spartan* as a prized exhibit.

The second Kirkintilloch-built VIC was launched in 1944, but never taken up by the Admiralty and became part of the Hays' fleet with the name *Kaffir*. She is seen here in 1949, at the end of the North Basin in Queen's Dock in Glasgow, with *Boer* and *Stormlight* (see page 35). In 1958 she was fitted with an underwater camera, echo sounding and other equipment and used in a live television broadcast on Loch Ness to search for the monster. Nessie chose not to appear. Converted to diesel in 1962, *Kaffir* was lost in almost Para Handy-like circumstances in September 1974. With the skipper and mate still ashore, she left her berth at Ayr's North Harbour and sailed a somewhat erratic course for a few hundred yards before going aground. The skipper got on board from a small boat, but the vessel was stuck fast and, despite a concerted attempt to save her, became a constructive loss. The engineer was charged with stealing the boat.

The 74 ton *Chindit* was the last puffer to be built by J. Hay & Sons at Kirkintilloch and her protracted launch in September 1945 suggested that somehow, something was reluctant to let her go. The system of holding the boat on the slip with two ropes, which were simultaneously severed by axes, had worked well for decades, but this time one of the axe shafts broke. With only one rope cut the boat slewed and ended up with the bow afloat and the stern stuck aground. After some embarrassment and hard labour, she was freed and floated the following day. *Chindit* seemed to have trouble with ropes because one night in 1960 she broke away from her moorings at Dunoon and bumped along the shore towards Kirn. Bent and battered, the damage, principally below the waterline, was too great to warrant repair and she was scrapped.

It is possible that some scows may have been built in the canal basin to the west of Kirkintilloch before 1902 when joinery contractor, Peter McGregor & Company, set up a boat building yard there. They had more space than the Hays so could build more than one vessel at a time and because they were not servicing their own fleet could take on a variety of work. One of their vessels was the 99 ton *Ardfern*, built for T. Dougall & R. Stirrat of Glasgow in 1910, and later owned by Warnock Brothers of Paisley one of the largest puffer operators. She seemed to have a propensity for going aground and even going under but like a prize fighter kept coming back for more. Seen here unloading coal at Kyleakin in the 1950s, she was scrapped at Arnott Young's yard at Dalmuir in 1966.

McGregor's yard closed in 1921 shortly after the 114 ton *Starfinch* was launched. She was the yard's second last boat, one of four lighters built for E. H. Bennett & Company of Newport, Monmouthshire. At 75 feet they were too long for the canal locks and so they made their maiden voyage down to Bowling with the bow section in the hold, to be attached at Scott's yard once they got to the river. Bennett sold the four boats soon after taking delivery of them, although only the *Starfinch* came back to the Clyde where she was operated by a number of owners before J. Hay & Sons bought her in 1950. Less than a month after this picture was taken at Princes Dock, in November 1952, she got into difficulties sailing between Tobermory and Barra with a cargo of coal. She was taken in tow, but sank.

During 1912 and 1913 McGregor's yard launched eight lighters with names beginning 'Innis' for the Coasting Motor Shipping Company. Like *Starfinch* they were too long for the canal (74 feet) and had to have the bow section attached at Bowling. What made them unusual was that they were all fitted with 'motor' engines. Such power systems were relatively new and so a number of different types were used: *Innishowen*, seen here, was one of two boats (the other was *Innisclora*) equipped with a two cylinder Kromhout 'hot bulb' engine. The 'Innis' boats were not a success, to some extent because the men who operated them struggled with the new technology, and they were all sold by the early 1920s. *Innishowen* went to Danish owners who renamed her *Eva Petersen*.

Although she looked like a puffer *Clydegate* was actually a motor-driven tanker and only ever carried one type of cargo - fuel oil. She was built at Grangemouth in 1923 for the Anglo-American Oil Company, the forerunner of Esso. She, and the older *Perfection*, a product of McGregor's Kirkintilloch yard, carried oil to coastal and canal-side customers. *Clydegate* is seen here above the Cloberhill Locks to the west of Glasgow with the crewman, who had probably been helping to work the locks, using the derrick to swing back aboard. This way of getting between boat and bank was common and although it would no doubt contravene today's health and safety strictures it saved a lot of time and tricky manoeuvring. The practice can be seen in the film *The Maggie* when two of the crew go ashore for a spot of poaching.

Kirkintilloch was not the only place on the Forth & Clyde Canal where boats were built. In the late 19th century William Burrell & Son (of Burrell Collection fame) constructed a number of lighters at a yard close to the Hamilton Hill basin, the original terminal of the canal's Glasgow branch before it was extended to Port Dundas. One of their vessels was the 70 ton, steel-hulled *Ashdale Glen,* seen here at Inveraray Pier. She was built in 1893 for John G. Frew and named after an Arran beauty spot. She had a number of owners in her time and was broken up in 1933.

William Burrell also built vessels beside the central basin of Port Dundas, at a yard which was later operated by William Jack & Company. They were one of the principal traders on the canal whose fleet at the start of the First World War consisted of ten scows and five steam lighters. One of their boats, built at Port Dundas and launched in October 1900, was the *Arab*, seen here working through Lock 16 at Camelon, Falkirk, about 1905. She is loaded with coal and operating with an open hold, a common practice on the canal, but one which, as can be seen, afforded very little freeboard. This suggests that she was not expected to go beyond the confined, and generally calm water of the canal or Grangemouth Docks

The principal canal-side yard in the Glasgow Area was the one where the story began in 1857, Kelvin Dock, Maryhill. One of its products, the *Hafton*, was an 81 ton vessel built in 1910. She is seen here fourteen years later at Ardrishaig on the Crinan Canal. Latterly she was owned and skippered by Alexander McLean. In September 1933 he was running coal between Bowling and Mull, discharging at a number of places in between, when the boat sprang a leak crossing the Firth of Lorne. The crew fired flares and sounded the horn, but failed to attract attention. With the engine compartment filling with water, they took to their small boat and stood off fearing a boiler explosion. *Hafton* sank. After spending an exhausting night on the open water the men came ashore on Seil Island.

The Kelvin Dock's history is closely associated with two families the Swans and the McNicols. David Swan, who became the first provost of the Burgh of Maryhill in 1856, took over the yard in the 1830s and with his sons worked it until 1893. In 1921, when the dock's last puffers, *Logan* and *Kype*, were launched, the yard manager was William McNicol and his brother Charles was a shipwright. They took over the yard in 1923 and although building no more puffers, continued to work at Kelvin Dock until 1949. The *Logan* and *Kype* were 98 ton vessels built for J. R. Dickson and Company to carry loads of up to 120 tons. *Logan*, seen here in Princes Dock, Glasgow, was latterly owned by the Warnock Brothers of Paisley. She foundered near Loch Aline in 1962.

Next to J. & J. Hay the largest lighter operator was the Greenock-based firm of Ross & Marshall. It was formed in 1872 by Alexander Ross, a coal merchant and lighter owner, and James Marshall who ran a stevedoring business. In the early days they moved offices a number of times from Cross Shore Street, to Cathcart Street and Dock Breast, all the time building up their fleet and expanding the business. They constructed a slipway and engine shop at Main Street then took over an adjoining slip, giving them the capacity to build and repair their own and other vessels. Much of the company's business was in servicing ships moored at the Tail of the Bank and they were also contracted to supply coal and water to naval vessels. One of the boats used as a water tanker was *Mellite*, built in 1889 and seen here in 1949. She had been kept working throughout the Second World War when the company managed a varied fleet of over 300 vessels for the Ministry of Transport.

Ross & Marshall's distinctive funnel colouring of red, topped with a narrow black band, a broad white band and a black top is not seen at its best on the stubby lum of this motor vessel. The company bought her in 1963 and called her *Limelight*, a name given to a number of their vessels. Originally built as the *Cristo* at Wivenhoe, Essex, in 1916 she had a number of owners, and was re-engined in 1958, before coming to Ross & Marshall. At 140 tons, 89 feet long, 19 feet in the beam and drawing 9 feet she was more akin to a coaster, but she shared the fate of many a puffer. In October 1966, while entering Port Ellen, Islay, with a cargo of bricks and bagged lime, she went aground on a rock known as Sgeir Thraghaidh. Bad weather thwarted all attempts at salvage and after two days *Limelight* was abandoned.

Starlight was a 91 ton vessel launched for Ross & Marshall at Ferguson Brothers' yard, Port Glasgow, in January 1937. She is seen here, in February 1956, aground in the Clyde, as if re-enacting the scene in *The Maggie* (see page 10). Ten years later she made her own screen debut when she was used in a second BBC Scotland black & white television series of the *Vital Spark* starring Roddy MacMillan as Para Handy. Like *Saxon* before her, *Starlight's* moment of glory turned out to be her last and she was withdrawn and scrapped in 1967. Her sister ship, *Skylight* which was sold in 1967 and renamed *Sitka*, was also used as the *Vital Spark* in the first television series to be made in colour. She fared little better than her predecessors, sinking beside the quay wall in Bowling Harbour. Although she was raised and taken to Greenock, she never sailed again.

Ross & Marshall took a step up from the coasting trade in 1921 with two ships of 800 tons operated by a subsidiary company, the Light Shipping Company. It was a short lived venture and the ships, *Raylight* and *Arclight*, were disposed of after a dozen years. The name *Raylight* reappeared in the late 1930s on a traditional steam lighter. She is seen here with the American aircraft carrier *Franklin D. Roosevelt*, in the background. Modifications to the carrier's appearance, made in the autumn of 1955, place the picture some time before that date.

A new *Raylight*, a 177 ton motor vessel, was launched from Scott & Company's Greenock yard in September 1963. Ten years later, on Christmas Day, she lost power and drifted on to the eastern shore of Jura. She was salvaged, but in August 1975, while heading light ship from Skye to Kilroot in Northern Ireland to load salt, she struck Highland Rock off Larne in thick fog and sank. The crew were rescued.

Seen here at the Dunardry Locks on the Crinan Canal is the third boat to bear the name *Moonlight*. She was a 164 ton steam lighter built in 1952 by W. J. Yarwood & Sons at Northwich, Cheshire. She was sold in 1966 and replaced by a fourth *Moonlight*, a 200 ton motor vessel which had been built in 1961 as the *Paullgate*. She foundered in heavy seas off the Isle of Man in September 1970 when her cargo of rock salt shifted. Only two of the four man crew survived. The second *Moonlight*, originally the Larne-built *Ormsa*, had suffered a similar fate. In August 1948, while on passage to Glasgow with a cargo of granite chips from Loch Fyne, she was caught by heavy weather off Ardlamont Point and sank. Only one member of the crew survived.

The 166 ton *Stormlight*, seen here at Glasgow's Custom House Quay in 1960, was built by W. J. Yarwood & Sons, at Northwich, in 1957 and launched by a great granddaughter of James Marshall, one of the company's founders. She was intended as a motor vessel, but in an early bout of uncertainty over Middle East oil supplies, the company changed its mind and fitted her with a traditional steam engine, converting her to diesel in 1969. She was a more modern craft in other ways with central heating, electric light and a small cabin with wardrobe and a bed light for each member of the crew - luxury indeed compared to the cramped, lightless, communal quarters crammed into the bow section of the early boats. Her fate, however, was not untypical: she ran aground at the entrance to Craighouse, Jura, in December 1973. The crew were taken off by the Islay lifeboat, but instead of the incoming tide freeing the boat as expected, the rocks held her fast and she became a total loss.

Ross & Marshall usually gave their boats names ending in 'light' although there were some early variations, like *Lucullite* (a black limestone often used, polished, for ornamental purposes). She was built at the company's Greenock yard in 1899 and remained in their fleet for twenty years before being sold to the Paisley-based Warnock Brothers. She is seen here in their colours at General Terminus Quay, Glasgow, being loaded with coal. Puffers often carried coal and some had a 'thief hole' in the bulkhead between the hold and engine room through which customers' coal was secretly shovelled to fire the boiler. This created a surplus of bunker coal, which the crew could then sell or trade. One boat, the Leith-built *Inchcolm* of the Mac Shipping Company, 'lost' twelve tons in transit from Troon to Coll in 1949. She developed a list in the Crinan Canal and so the skipper put in at Tobermory to trim his load. At the time there was a shortage of coal on Mull, so a local merchant's sudden ability to supply his customers raised suspicions, but nothing could be proved when the case came to court in Oban.

The 95 ton *Arran Rose*, seen here in Princes Dock, Glasgow, in 1949 spent almost as much of her working life on the east coast as the west. She was launched as *Garmoyle* in 1904 by William Denny & Sons at Dumbarton and was known in the trade to 'load by the heid' - out of trim, with the stern up and the bow down. Acquired after only three years by A. F. Henry & MacGregor of Leith she then moved north to the Dundee, Perth & London Shipping Company who renamed her *North Inch*. Working out of Dundee she traded up river to Perth or to east coast ports as far apart as Montrose and Berwick. She returned to the Clyde in 1922 when Colin McPhail bought her for his Shira Steamship Company. He called her *Stronshira*, but in 1946 her name was changed to *Arran Rose* when she became the property of the Arran Sea Transport & Supply Company. Four years later she was back on the Forth working for J. A. White of North Queensferry.

The first *Glencloy* was a wooden–hulled boat built in 1895 beside the river at Brodick by Adam Hamilton. His sons, George and Gavin, formed one of the best known owner operator companies on the Clyde, G. & G. Hamilton. Their second *Glencloy* - the first was sold in 1911 - was a 138 ton vessel built in 1930 by Scott & Sons of Bowling to Crinan Canal dimensions. She was converted from coal to oil burning in 1955 and instead of having a tall lum in front of the wheel house (as on the front cover) she emerged with the wheel house in front of a shorter funnel. She is seen here in this later guise in 1963, at Scarinish, Tiree. In the foreground are the wrecks of the schooner *Mary Stewart* (left) and the fishing boat *Thistle*. She was sold to Alexander McNeil & Co. of Greenock in 1966 and renamed *Glenholm*, but stranded at Cove in Loch Long the following year and was broken up.

G. & G. Hamilton's second boat was the *Invercloy*, launched in 1904 by the Larne Shipbuilding Company. The Brodick-based company reputedly worked their boats hard on the now familiar principal that when stationary, or running empty, they were not earning money - a policy that made the 'cloys' a familiar sight wherever puffers operated. The first *Invercloy* was replaced in 1934 by another boat of the same name built by Scott's of Bowling. She conformed to the 66 foot length required to navigate the Forth & Clyde Canal, but is seen here on the upper Clyde looking somewhat diminutive beside an ocean-going freighter. *Invercloy* was converted to oil burning and remained in service until 1967 when she was broken up at Dalmuir.

The 97 ton *Glenrosa* was built as *VIC 29* in 1944 by Isaac Pimblott & Sons of Northwich. She was renamed when she was bought by G. & G. Hamilton who amalgamated with Colin McPhail in 1948 to form a new company: Hamilton-McPhail. Ten years later, in January 1958, the boom defence vessel *HMS Barrington* was standing off Mull in thick fog when the crew of *Glenrosa* pulled alongside in their small boat. They had been taking a cargo of coal to Bunessan and had struck the rocky shore near Lochbuie. The naval vessel was there because only two days earlier her sister ship, *HMS Barcombe*, had crashed in exactly the same way as the puffer, her navigation instruments apparently affected by the magnetic pull of the mountains. No lives were lost, but both the *Barcombe* and *Glenrosa* were written-off.

Lady Bute, seen here in 1952, was originally the *Rivercloy*, a 100 ton vessel built in 1910 by the Larne Ship Building Company for G. & G. Hamilton and noted as being one of the fastest boats in the trade. She was sold to a Rothesay-based owner, F. Dewar, in 1952 and was also owned by Alexander McNeil of Greenock before being broken up at Troon about 1960. In the background is the Clyde steamer *Queen Mary II* which had her two funnels replaced by a single fatter one in 1957 when she was re-boilered at Barclay Curle's shipyard. She was withdrawn twenty years later and, after an unsuccessful campaign to keep her on the river as an exhibit of the Clyde's maritime traditions, she became a pub/restaurant on the Thames.

Despite being based in Northern Ireland, the Larne Shipbuilding Company established a reputation amongst Scottish lightermen for building good sea boats. *Jennie,* was one of their products, built in 1902 for Malcolm Campbell and skippered by his son Alex. His other son Duncan skippered a sister vessel, *Ormsa* which later became Ross & Marshall's *Moonlight* (2). They were 95 ton vessels which could carry up to 125 tons of cargo and were built to conform to the limits of the Forth & Clyde Canal. In February 1954 *Jennie* went aground on the north end of Eigg in thick fog. Another Larne-built boat, the *Lythe,* was sent to take off her cargo of coal, but she too grounded, and both vessels were lost.

The almost identical lines of *Petrel* and *Faithful* indicate that they were both products of the Larne Ship Building Company. *Petrel* was the older having been launched in 1897 for James Burrows who kept her in immaculate condition until his death in the 1930s. Her end came in April 1951 when Alexander McNeil was using her to dredge for sand off Cardross. An explosion in the engine room threw the skipper, the owner's 23 year old son Alexander, into the water about fifty feet from the boat. He was picked up in the dinghy by the two other crew members. They were rescued as they rowed toward Port Glasgow. *Faithful* was launched in 1906, and like *Petrel*, she could pass through the Forth & Clyde Canal, which was just as well because her original owners were based at St Monance, Fife - hence the Methil registration. By the 1920s she was working on the Clyde and was broken up at Port Glasgow in 1954.

VIC 7 was built in 1941 by D. R. Dunstan of Thorne in Yorkshire. After the war she was acquired by D. McCorquodale who named her *Lady Isle* after a small island off her home port of Troon. She is seen here about 1949. On 10 August 1956, she ran aground at the entrance to the harbour at Scarinish, Tiree, and was abandoned by her crew. Her relatively sheltered position raised hopes that she could be refloated, but attempts to pump her out were in vain and she was declared a wreck. She was quickly replaced by *VIC 9* which was also renamed *Lady Isle* and later converted to diesel. The actual island of Lady Isle claimed a puffer victim when J. Hay and Sons' *Cuban* ran aground one January night in 1955. The crew was rescued by the Troon lifeboat and the boat was salvaged by Hay's rescue squad who based themselves in a bird watchers' hut while they worked on the stranded vessel.

William Burke's *Cloch Lass* was built as *VIC 23* and had been operated by Ross & Marshall under the name *Limelight* until the late 1950s when they replaced her with the diesel coaster of the same name (see page 31). The ability of owners to update their fleets quickly and cheaply with these VIC boats after the war may well have prolonged the use of steam and delayed the introduction of diesel for a number of years. A later conflict helped to extend the life of *Cloch Lass* and another boat *Toward Lass*, the former *VIC 12*, which were used as tenders to the US Navy's Cold War Polaris submarine base in the Holy Loch. They were both upgraded and converted to diesel in the early 1960s, largely at American expense. A third 'Lassie', the *Cumbrae Lass*, formerly the *Pibroch*, (see page 46) remained as a steam vessel. *Cloch Lass* was broken up in 1969.

Puffers were generally used to carry any cargo their owners saw fit to put in their holds, but the 96 ton *Pibroch* had a single purpose, servicing the White Horse Distillery on Islay. Launched in 1923 by Scott's of Bowling she carried supplies to the distillery and brought barrels of whisky out. The epitome of Para Handy's 'smartest boat in the coasting trade' and sporting a white horse weathercock at her masthead, she was a regular on the Crinan Canal and is seen here in the sea lock at Ardrishaig. Sold in 1957 she was renamed *Texa*, and then *Cumbrae Lass* before being broken up at Arnott Young's Dalmuir yard in 1967. Her replacement was an 87 foot x 20 foot motor vessel, also named *Pibroch* which was launched for Scottish Malt Distillers Ltd by Scott's of Bowling in December 1956.

The demise of the traditional puffer gathered pace through the 1960s as more diesel coasters were built to replace them. Typical of these was *Glenfyne*, a 199 ton vessel built by Scott's of Bowling and launched in March 1965. She entered the fleet of a new company, Hay-Hamilton, formed in 1964 by the merger of Hamilton-McPhail and J. & J. Hay. The process of amalgamating the old companies continued in 1968 when Hay-Hamilton and Ross & Marshall formed an operating company, Glenlight Shipping, which carried the flag for coastal shipping until 1994. *Glenfyne* remained in their fleet until she was sold in 1987. She is seen here, above at Toberonochy, Luing, and, on the left, discharging coal at Uig, Skye.

The steam puffer had a couple of final flings. In 1969 Sir James Millar, former Lord Provost of Edinburgh, purchased the former fleet water tanker *VIC 27*, renamed her *Auld Reekie* and put her to use as a training vessel for youth clubs. She was later taken over by new owners who based her at Crinan and hired her out to holidaymakers, such as these, in 1982. She spent the summer of 1988 at the Glasgow Garden Festival as the *Vital Spark*, and was then cast in that role when BBC Scotland revived the Para Handy stories, with Gregor Fisher in the lead role.

Another puffer, *VIC 32*, was also converted for the tourist trade by a couple of enthusiasts, Nick and Rachel Walker, who based her at Crinan and from 1979 provided 'Highland Steamboat Holidays'. People were given options, they could wrestle with the wheel, get hot and sweaty in the engine room, handle ropes as a deck hand or just watch from a deck chair. The holidays came to an abrupt halt in 2004 when her boiler failed its inspection, but the subsequent award of a Heritage Lottery Fund grant raises hopes for the future. She is seen here at Crinan in 1993.